AF322688

Sam Wants to Get Married

Written by Samantha-Marie VanAlstyne

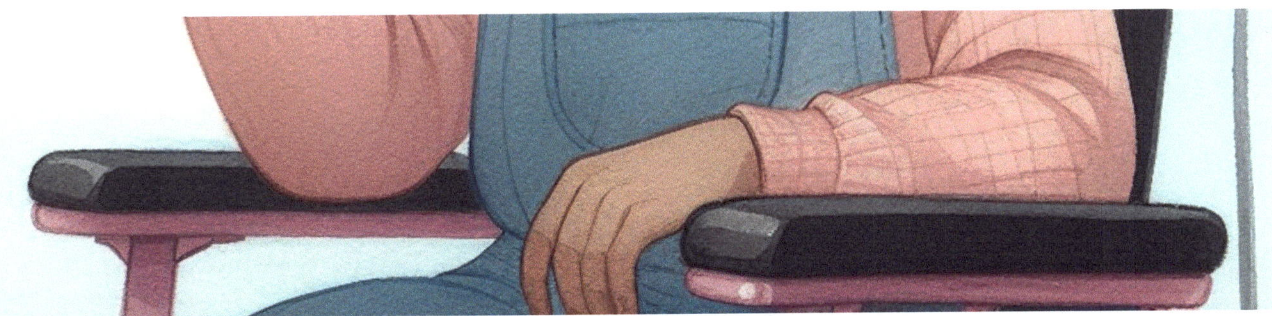

Hi, my name is Sam! Well, it's really Samantha, but I like Sam better. It's nice to see you again!

I want you to meet Jordan. He's a very special person in my life. He even asked me to marry him!

But there's a problem with that. It has to do with our disabilities.

Jordan and I both have disabilities, but they're different. Jordan can walk with a crutch, but I use my wheelchair every day.

SSI
Both of our disabilities make it hard to work. So, we both get help from the government. This is called SSI.

SSI
Every month, the government sends us money. This helps us pay for things we need, like food and a place to live.

You might be wondering, "What does getting married have to do with money?" It's okay if you're confused. Let me explain.

The government has a rule. If we get married, we might lose our SSI money. That's a problem.
GOVERNMENT RULEBOOK

The government decides who gets money based on how much they have. If you have too much, you can't get SSI.

If Jordan and I get married, our money would be combined. That means we might not have enough to pay for what we need.

We're planning a commitment ceremony on Halloween 2026. It's like a wedding, but we can't legally get married without losing our help.

Why is this a problem? If we marry, we could lose our support, and that would make life much harder.

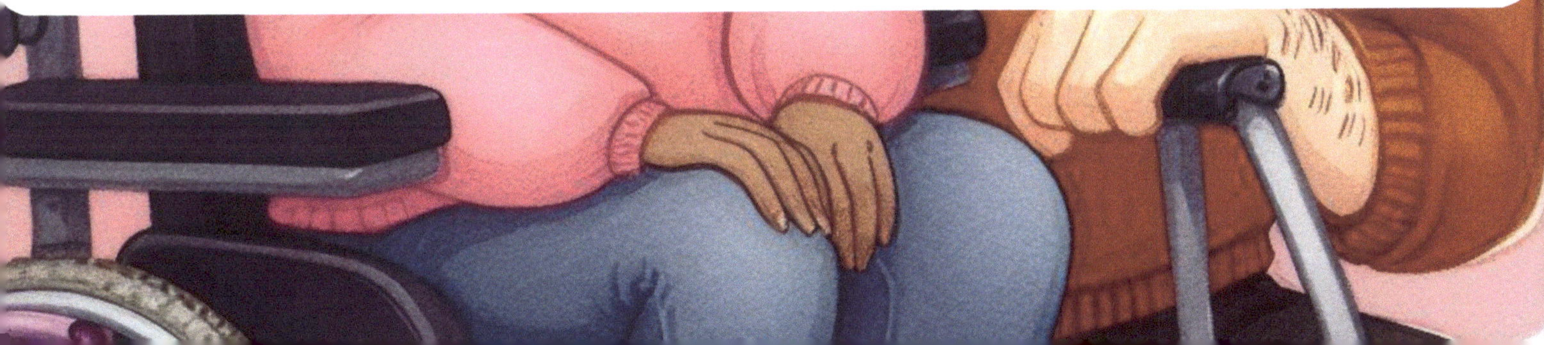

I love Jordan and he loves me.
We want to get married and
still have enough money to live

Many people with disabilities face this same problem. They can't marry without losing their help.

Love without limits
love without
Can you imagine not being able to marry the person you love? It's not fair.

RENT
MARRIAGE
Some people even stop living together because of this rule. They love each other, but they can't afford to lose their support.

MARRIAGE EQUALITY FOR DISABLED ACT.
Jordan and I dream of a world where we can marry and still get the help we need. Wouldn't that be great?

If we get married, we don't want to lose the help we need to live. We want both love and support.

DiSABLed rights are Human rights.
There's a new law being proposed. It's called the Marriage Equality for Disabled Adults Act.

LOVE WITHOUT LIMITS
HOLD LINTS
SUPP
MARI
EQUA
This law would let people with disabilities marry without losing their help from the government. Not many people know about it yet, but it could make a big difference!

We talk about this law a lot. We hope that one day it will pass, and things will change for people like us.
LAW PASSED!

We're not alone in this. Many people with disabilities want the same thing: to be loved and supported.
WELCOME HOME

There are people who are working hard to change the rules. They want to make sure that people like us can get married and still get help.

Even though it's hard, we never stop trying. Jordan says that change takes time.

Jordan and I don't live together yet. We may not be able to, because of the rules about marriage and money.

We want to live together, but we need the rules to change first. That's why we hope the Marriage Equality for Disabled Adults Act will pass.

Sometimes things are tough, but we keep working for what's right. We never give up on our dreams.

Jordan reminds me of all the good things in our lives. We have love, friends, and hope.

Together, we believe things can change. Love should never be limited.

People all over are helping us.
They want to make things fair
for everyone with disabilities.

I know that if we all work together, we can make a change. People should be able to love and still get the help they need.

I'm Sam, and this is our story of hoping for love without limitation

Acknowledgments

Firstly, thank you to my partner Jordan for helping inspire this book. I wouldn't want to do life without you. I love you! Secondly, thank you to my mom Janet for the idea to write a new book to help fund our ceremony. Finally, thank you to everyone who has continued to support my work as an author.

Review
If you enjoyed the book, please leave a positive review on whichever website you purchased the book. Reviews help other readers find the book

Follow the author on social media
Facebook: https://www.facebook.com/samvanalsynewrites
Instagram: https://www.instagram.com/author.samanthavanalstyne
Twitter: https://www.x.com/VanAlstyne_Sam